# Soccer at the Park

Story by Jenny Giles
Illustrations by Scott Fraser

Tim looked at the big boys
playing soccer.
They kicked the ball
up and down the park.

Tim said,

"Can I play with you?

I like playing soccer."

"No," said a big boy.
"You are too little
  to play soccer with us."

Tim went away.

He looked back at the big boys.

A boy ran
and kicked the ball.

The ball went up,
and it came all the way down
to Tim.

Tim ran to the ball,

and he kicked it back.

The ball went up, up, up,

all the way back

to the big boys.

The boys looked at Tim.

"Come on," said a big boy.
"You can play with us.
You are good at soccer,
for a little boy."

And Tim ran to play soccer
with the big boys.